Bugs Aren't So Scary!

Discover, Learn, Explore

**Includes Story,
Bug Encyclopedia
& Fun Activities**

By Ambrose Martin

Flash Studios LLC
Copyright April 15, 2024

Hello!

Welcome to the wonderful world of bugs!

Meet the Beetles

Beetles come in all shapes and sizes. Some are big, some are small, but all are friendly!

The Ant Family

Ants may be tiny, but they are mighty workers! They build homes and gather food for their colony

Fluttering Butterflies

Butterflies are like flying rainbows! They flutter gracefully from flower to flower, spreading joy.

Spider Friends

Spiders may spin webs, but they are also skilled hunters who help keep pesky bugs in check.

The Buzz of Bees

Bees are busy bees indeed! They make sweet honey and pollinate flowers, helping them grow.

Caterpillar Tales

Caterpillars may start small, but they grow into beautiful butterflies! It's a magical transformation.

Grasshopper Jumps

Grasshoppers love to hop and play! They leap high in the air, showing off their acrobatic skills.

Firefly Magic

Fireflies light up the night sky with their twinkling glow. It's like having stars on the ground!

Dragonfly Delight

Dragonflies zip and zoom through the air, their colorful wings shimmering in the sunlight.

Bugs, Are our Friends

Bugs may make you squirm, but guess what? They're like tiny superheroes! Each bug has its own special role in nature.

The end...or is it just the beginning of our bug-filled adventures? Remember, bugs aren't so scary after all!

Bugs Aren't So Scary! Discover, Learn, Explore!
Bug Encyclopedia

Beetles are the largest group of insects, with over 350,000 different species. They come in all shapes, sizes, and colors, making them one of the most diverse groups in the insect world.

Ants are social insects that live in colonies and work together to build intricate nests, gather food, and care for their young. There are over 12,000 species of ants found worldwide.

Butterflies are beloved for their beauty and grace.

These winged wonders undergo a remarkable transformation from caterpillar to butterfly through the process of metamorphosis.

Spiders are skilled hunters that play a vital role in controlling insect populations. They spin silk webs to catch prey and use venom to subdue their meals.

Bees are essential pollinators responsible for fertilizing flowers and enabling the reproduction of many plant species. They also produce honey, beeswax, and royal jelly.

Caterpillars are the larval stage of butterflies and moths. They have voracious appetites and spend most of their time eating and growing before transforming into adults.

Grasshoppers are known for their ability to jump long distances using their powerful hind legs. They are herbivores that feed on grasses and other vegetation.

Fireflies are famous for their bioluminescent light, which they use to communicate and attract mates. Their nighttime displays are a magical sight to behold.

Dragonflies are agile predators that hunt other flying insects in mid-air. With their large eyes and swift flight, they are masters of the skies

We hope you've enjoyed this journey through the Bug Encyclopedia! May it inspire you to continue exploring the fascinating world of insects and appreciate the vital roles they play in our ecosystem. Happy bug hunting!

How to Make a Firefly Trap

Materials Needed

- Empty glass jar with a lid
- Poking tool (such as a nail or small drill)
- Battery-powered LED light (optional)
- Tape (optional)
- Twine or string (optional)

Instructions

1. Prepare your jar: Ensure the glass jar is clean and dry. Remove the lid and set it aside.

2. Create air holes: Use a poking tool to create small air holes in the lid of the jar. These holes will allow air to circulate inside the jar while keeping the fireflies safely contained.

3. Add a light source (optional): If you want to attract fireflies to your trap, place a battery-powered LED light inside the jar. You can tape the light to the inside of the lid or place it at the bottom of the jar.

4. Secure the lid: Once the light is in place, securely screw the lid onto the jar. Make sure it is tight enough to prevent any fireflies from escaping.

5. Set up your trap: Place the jar in an area where you've seen fireflies before, such as near bushes, trees, or open fields. Fireflies are attracted to light, so they may be drawn to your trap if you've added a light source.

6. Wait patiently: Leave the jar out overnight or during dusk, when fireflies are most active. Check the trap periodically to see if any fireflies have been caught.

7. Release the fireflies: Once you've captured some fireflies, carefully unscrew the lid of the jar and release them back into the wild. Be gentle and handle the fireflies with care to avoid injuring them.

8. Optional: Decorate your trap: If you'd like, you can decorate the outside of the jar with twine, string, or stickers to make it more visually appealing.

Remember, it's important to respect nature and handle fireflies gently. Enjoy observing these magical insects in their natural habitat, and have fun with your firefly trapping adventure!